*Listed on the **Selling Power Best Books for Sales Success in 2013***

LEADERSHIP SALES COACHING

Executive Summary

JASON FORREST

Author of *40-Day Sales Dare* and *Creating Urgency*

For information or bulk orders, contact:
info@forrestpg.com

ForrestPG.com

Published by MJS Press
Printed in the U.S.A.

International Standard Book Number: 978-0-9887523-3-7

WHAT **PEOPLE ARE SAYING**

"*Leadership Sales Coaching* is so much more than a book! It's a field guide for sales coaches to mark up, dog ear, and use in the heat of battle. 'Some people watch what happens, others wonder what happens.' This book helps managers make it happen!"
—Rob Bowman, *President, Charter Homes & Neighborhoods*

"This approach has never been done before! Finally a 'training' book that provides so much more than just theory. Finally a tactical guide that transforms sales managers into sales coaches and equips them to lead their team members to X-Factor success. Finally a blueprint for homebuilders and other big-ticket sales organizations to change the way they hire and do business. Leadership Sales Coaching takes an approach that has never been done before. And it's an absolute must-have."
—Liesel Cooper, *Senior Vice President, MDC Holdings, Inc.*

"Jason Forrest has taken the luck out of selling with a program that places the responsibility where it belongs—with the sales department. Rather than a day-long seminar that hypes sales teams and then leaves them high and dry, Jason's program and products ensure a long-term commitment to learning new methods. Defining the role of the coach keeps the lessons fresh and never allows complacency. I am convinced Jason is redefining the sales process."
—Jay Moss, *Chief Marketing Officer, Woodside Homes*

"This book teaches the habits, practices, and strategies of the world's best sales coaches."
—Steve Greig, *Owner, AutoMAXX*

A Note From Jason:

Leaders,

What you're seeing here is an executive summary of *Leadership Sales Coaching: Transforming from Manager to Coach*. My goal is to sell you on the philosophy that sales coaches are more effective for increasing sales results and building a positive company culture than sales managers. What's the difference between a manager and a coach? Give me one hour of your time to read this book and find out. And remember, this contains only a taste of what you'll find in the full version.

If you believe in the philosophy when you've completed this, buy the book or give us a call to start the transformation.

Here's to earning what you're worth!

Jason Forrest

Definitions to Lead By

LEADER
*"A person that you follow to a place
you would not go on your own."*
—Joel Barker

PRINCIPLE
"Specific guideline/rule to achieve success."
—Dictionary.com

Contents

PART ONE

Introduction to *Leadership Sales Coaching*

"When you change the way you look at things, the things you look at change."
–Heisenberg Uncertainty Principle

Introduction to *Leadership Sales Coaching*

I nformation without a change in behavior is useless. The most effective, longest-lasting way to change behavior is to change beliefs. If we can change what people see (and therefore, what they believe), we can change how they behave. Because beliefs drive emotions, emotions drive behaviors, and behaviors drive results. This belief permeates my approach to everything—my work, my life, and all of the in-between.

It's not about working harder; it's about thinking differently.

Instead of just seminars (which teach behaviors) I believe in coaching, which challenges current beliefs and develops new beliefs and then follows up with experiential training. Seminars offer a short-term hype, but true training occurs over the long-term and coaches beliefs. If the beliefs line up, the behaviors will follow. And with changed behaviors come changed results.

As a sales coach, you are in a unique position to improve your sales professionals' lives. By influencing the way they think and leading them to see things differently, you can hold your team members accountable to being more than they believe is possible, and (ever important in our business) increasing their earnings.

This book may not be for you if:

• You would rather manage tasks than improve lives.
• You include Starbucks drinks as one of your top motivational tools.
• You think your role is to be a liaison between sales professionals and management.
• You would rather make excuses than take success into your own hands.
• You don't care how your sales professionals get sales results, just that they get them.

On the other hand, this book is for you if:

• You are a sales professional who would like to become a sales coach.
• You are a good sales manager and would like to be a better one.
• You want to create an atmosphere where your sales pros want to get time with you because they know it makes them better (and earns them more money).
• You want to truly make a difference in people's lives.
• You want to lead, communicate, and maintain a standard.
• You want to get buy-in from team members, peers, and managers.
• You want to know your team members—what makes them tick and what ticks them off.
• You want to communicate effectively, use your time wisely, and create self-assurance in your people.

And most of all—if you want to build a culture where sales professionals believe that what they do matters, this book is for you.

What we believe, how we feel, how we think, and how we see ourselves, have more influence over our sales success than what we do. And the coaching we get along the way makes all the difference. You are in a position to be that leader for someone. Will you accept the task?

Here's to coaching your sales professionals to earn what they're worth!

Your sales coach,
Jason

"A leader is a person that you follow to a place you would not go to on your own."
—Joel Barker

You're Either Leading or Yielding

You're either leading or yielding. True sales professionals, sales coaches, and executives lead. Joel Barker's definition of a leader is at the core of my Leadership Selling, Leadership Sales Coaching, and Leadership Sales Culture philosophies and training programs.

Leadership Selling trains sales professionals to create interest in the uninterested and to convince the just-looking prospect to buy from them today over all alternatives.

Leadership Sales Coaching trains sales managers (coaches) to *lead sales professionals to do the things they don't want to do so they can earn what they want to earn.*

Leadership Sales Culture trains executives to transform companies into sales organizations.

Each program goes back to this concept that a leader is a person you follow to a place you would not go on your own. Without a sales professional's leadership, customers delay decisions on products that will improve their lives. Sales professionals may not reach their potential to earn what they're worth without their sales coach's accountability. And a company may not achieve sustainable profits without executive oversight.

In this book, we're focusing on the sales coach's aspect of this theory—leading sales professionals to do the things they don't want to do so that they can earn what they want to earn.

Paradox of Success

Ost likely, what your boss, peers, and team members expect you to do is exactly the opposite of what you need to do to be successful in your role. What's more harmful, is if what others expect from you, is what you expect from yourself.

When you signed up for this job, you were told that you were in charge of the sales results for your company. The variables that you use to achieve those results are known as the nine P's of marketing. On the graphic below, count which P's are covered in your job description and/or the socially-accepted expectations of your role.

If you're like most of my clients (at least when I first sign with them), most of your answers fall on the left side. The left side includes things like what your marketing materials look like, whether the colors on your billboards are just right, and whether your store has the right lighting. This is the paradox—the aspects that will increase your sales results are those on the right.

This book came about because I kept seeing job descriptions and titles that lumped marketing (which encompasses the P's on the left) and sales (which focuses more on the P's on the right) together. That dangerous lumping practice is also what I saw in my experience as a national sales trainer for a large public homebuilder. Christine, a sales professional, asked if I could come out to her office and shadow her the next time I was in town. I did and we spent three hours together. I coached her—passing along the sales processes and techniques that had worked for me when I was in her shoes. Two weeks later, she called again. She said, "When can you come out again? I just made three grand in commission creating a sale off of what you taught me. I want to learn more!"

When I asked about her sales manager, she said, "Oh, she doesn't do those things. She helps with the paperwork side...makes sure I have enough brochures at the office...negotiates deals."

Though she didn't know it, Christine told me that her manager did the P's on the left. At that moment, I realized that I was on to something—what I did with Christine was the future job description of a sales manager. And a sales manager would actually be a sales coach.

But I knew it would be difficult to convince builders of my controversial idea—builders were benefitting from a great housing market and stayed competitive as long as those P's on the left were in line. Sales managers were six-figure admins and that was just fine with everyone. They didn't want to change. What's more, it was a good market, so they didn't *have* to change.

When the market tanked, the status quo wasn't going to cut it anymore. Though people needed the P's on the left to be in line, what they really needed was to focus on the P's on the right—the ones that could set them apart from everyone else and earn them a greater percentage of the shrinking market share. And that's exactly what this book is about.

Those P's on the right (the P's of sales) are what the modern sales coach needs to be focused on in order to succeed—in good markets and bad.

If you accept what I'm saying and pursue this new way of thinking, be prepared to be lonely—because it ain't always popular. Your bosses are conditioned to believe that success lies in the P's on the left. So that's what they hold you accountable to. Other department heads are blinded to the P's on the right. So they'll have no problem complaining to you about the P's on the left and will expect you to be in meetings that cover details you don't need to be involved in.

Even your team members will expect your advice and leadership on the things on the left. They might even rebel when you bring up the P's on the right. Everyone around you will create so much noise about things that don't actually make you meet your sales goals. They'll make it socially unacceptable to be the coach you want to be.

Don't get me wrong. The product, promotional strategies, packaging, production, position, and place absolutely need to be in line. But this book is about the P's on the right because the P's on the left do little more than keep you in the game. But to win the game, you have to dominate the P's on the right.

Your **people, process,** and **presentation** are what will help you achieve, increase market share, and outdo your competition. As I write, 100% of my clients are beating their market. It's not because they're producing an extraordinary iProduct that sets them apart from everyone else. It's because they see sales differently and they coach their sales professionals to be the best version of themselves.

It's about learning how to grow your sales professionals and improve their sales processes and presentations. And trust me—they'll all come around. When your managers see market share increase, when other department heads aren't feeling the pressure that comes with low sales, and when sales professionals start making more money, they'll see the light. They'll believe.

PARADOX OF SUCCESS

P's of MARKETING	P's of SALES
• Product	• People
• Price	• Process
• Promotion	• Presentation
• Position	
• Packaging	
• Place	

Remember Your Purpose

Managers get lost in the details.

———————

Coaches remember their purpose.

T hink of the most influential people in your life: the coaches, teachers, and mentors who see more in you than you see in yourself. Chances are, there are one or two special people you'll always credit with pushing you—challenging you to achieve more than you thought possible. Get this: Now your job is to be that person to each of your team members. Why? Because the purpose of a coach is to *lead sales professionals to do the things they don't want to do so they can earn what they want to earn.*

Big ticket sales professionals want to make big money. If they didn't, they wouldn't sign up for the gig. They know they're going to have to work harder than a Monday through Friday, fixed-income employee. They choose that course because they want to have unlimited earning potential.

So why do they often fall short of their potential? The truth is that even though sales professionals want to make the money, they don't always know (or want to do) what it's going to take. In either case, a coach is there to lead them to do those uncomfortable things on a consistent basis so that they can earn what they want to earn.

The toughest aspect of any leader is to get his or her people to exceed their own expectations. Why? Because every sales professional has a subconscious limit on what they believe they can achieve and what is possible in their given circumstances. Until Roger Bannister broke it in 1954, the four-minute mile was considered impossible for runners. As soon as Bannister demonstrated that it was possible, others quickly followed suit. The truth is, people made it impossible because of their beliefs. They defended its impossibility adamantly. When people are locked on to a particular belief, they will do whatever they need to do in order to live up to that. Even to the point where they will defend their beliefs and get defensive when their beliefs are challenged. Once sales professionals reach what they believe is possible, they stop.

When people don't do something to earn what they're worth, it's because of one or more of the following:

1. They don't know how *(on a logical/ behavioral level)*.

2. They don't know why they should do it and/or lack confidence that they are capable *(on a beliefs level)*.

3. They have a reluctance/fear *(on an emotional level)* that keeps them from doing the appropriate behavior.

4. They've had past or current conditioning from coaches, parents, significant others, cultural influences, or educators *(on a programming level)*.

And that's why they need you. They need you to lead them toward personal growth and self-efficacy. It's not as easy (for you or for them) as saying, "Here's what I need you to do" and then leaving them alone to do it. Most human beings just aren't wired to achieve their potential by themselves. Along with instruction, they need follow-through, accountability, and maintenance.

Remember that you're dealing with their past coaching, fears, programming, support systems at home, etc. And it's a challenge. BUT precisely because it is a challenge, it is also extremely rewarding.

Remember that your purpose is bigger than just getting strong sales results.

Remember Your Purpose

It's a key that will guide you through frustrating times. Sometimes, it's going to seem like people just aren't getting it. Sometimes, it's going to seem like team members aren't interested in exceeding their own expectations. But it all becomes worth it when even one person's life is more fulfilled because of you. When you start to have those successes, you'll be able to say, "Okay, I'll take the rest of the crap." It all becomes worth it with one good success.

You want to improve your life. Your sales pros want to improve theirs. Tap into that desire because if you can lead them to get what they want out of this career, then you yourself will get what you want out of it. As you challenge yourself with the ideas and tasks ahead, think, "How will my life be better by doing this? How can I improve things for my family?

This stuff matters. But it ain't easy. And in order to have those moments, you've got to be a coach who leads sales professionals, maintains the coaching, and creates self-assurance.

Every principle from here on out is about you achieving that purpose. Ultimately, that purpose comes down to improving lives. You will be the difference.

Additional Reading

Management Challenges of the 21st Century, by Peter Drucker

People Principle, by Ron Willingham

PART TWO

Coaching to Win

Coach, Don't Manage

__Managing__ is what you do to someone.

__Coaching__ is what you do for them.

I f I had my way, any reference to *manager* or *director* would be eliminated from your business cards and replaced with a title that identifies you with preparing, educating, inspiring, and holding your people accountable to what they're worth. The title would be *sales coach.*

Even the definitions for manager and coach evoke very different feelings: One is associated with control and limitations, the other with inspiration and progress.

A **manager** is "a person who has *control* or direction of an institution, business, etc., or of a part, division, or phase of it." Did you notice the word "control" in that definition? That causes feelings of oppression and domination. And for good reason—its synonyms are *hold back, bridle, check, constrain, repress, corner, smother, and subdue.*

Wow.

On the other hand, a **coach** is "a person who trains an athlete or a team of athletes." Think of your people as corporate athletes—people who get paid based on their performance and contributions to the team.

Would you rather control or lead? Constrain or inspire? Be exhausted or fulfilled? If those questions were easy to answer, keep reading—this book is for you. If you hesitated on any of them, call me. Right away. Because we've got some work to do.

It's exhausting to try to find ways to force people to get the job done. On the other hand, coaching is energizing and fulfilling because you know you are leading people to achieve more than they could accomplish by themselves.

Coach, Don't Manage

Action Items

1. Go through the synonyms for *manage* and *coach* and circle the words that most describe you and/or your sales leader(s) on each side.

2. Add them up and determine what percentage of your team's style is like a coach and what is like a manager.

3. Start thinking of your team members as corporate athletes and your sales leaders as sales coaches!

COACH, DON'T MANAGE

TO MANAGE:	TO COACH:
to control in action or use	*to give instruction or advice to in the capacity of a coach; instruct.*
• dominate	• mentor
• boss	• teach
• call the shots	• train
• command	• educate
• manipulate	• prepare
• control	• guide
• regulate	• inspire
• take over	• advise
• constrain	• improve
• rule	• develop
• restrain	• cultivate

"The more I practice, the luckier I get."
—Jerry Barber, golfer

Be on Offense

Managers hear about the sale after it happens.

Coaches strategize before the sale.

D efense is "An action of defending from or resisting an attack," an "attempt to protect/defend against opposition" or a "barrier against attack." When leaders of sales teams manage defensively, they are just trying to survive in the market. Offense is "the action of attacking," or "the team or players who are attempting to score or advance the ball."

Rather than simply putting her head down and hoping for the best, an offensive coach attacks, makes things happen, and strategizes the sale long before it becomes a sale.

I talk to clients all the time who try to tell me that they take this kind of proactive approach. But when I dig a little deeper, I find that they're sitting in their offices, taking phone calls from sales professionals, and talking about customer offers.

During those calls, they have one overriding goal: Get the deal to the finish line without getting creamed on profit margins. In football, this approach would be like being in a goal-line stance, knowing that you're about to get scored on, and doing all you can just to hold your opponents to a field goal.

On the other hand, coaching offensively means considering the people (their attitudes, beliefs, and fears) and the process (coaching sales professionals through where the sale stopped, what decision needs to happen to move this prospect forward, and how you can improve the sales professionals' presentations).

An important aspect of gaining the win is strategizing the sale before it happens. Find out when your sales professionals are having their prospect appointments, and talk through the exact process and presentation (play) they plan to use to make the sale happen. Talk through potential objections and how the sales professional is going to handle those. Before you call the play, you make a strategy. You say, "So the Joneses are coming in. What will you do in x, y, z situation?" This is a great time to role-play so that the sales pro can confidently execute the play that you've agreed upon. This gives the sales pro the highest probability for success (rather than having them make it up as they go along).

There just aren't enough market sales (sales that would happen with or without the persuasive efforts of sales coaches and sales professionals) for us to make our goals each month. Market sales can be counted by an admin. Six-figure employees should be making x-factor sales happen.

You can either count sales by managing defensively, or you can create sales by moving the ball forward, one coaching call/strategy at a time. Choose wisely—your company's success (and your own) depend on it!

"Beyond the finish line, I'd heard from so many people [that] maintenance is the hardest thing. [I used to think], 'Try losing 200 pounds.' But maintenance really is a lifetime."
—Erik Chopin, Biggest Loser

Be the 66%

Managers focus on "get-fixed quick" solutions.

Coaches focus on sustainability.

E ven after you equip your sales pros with all the information they need, they, like Erik, will need someone in their lives to hold them accountable.

People can be afraid of that word—accountability. They think it's going to mean someone's breathing down their neck, shining a spotlight on their every misstep, and making them feel they're just not enough. It doesn't have to be that way though. When you gain a "want to" relationship with your sales pros, they will see accountability as something that increases their paychecks and leads them to achieve more satisfaction in their careers. They will want you to play the role of coach in their lives.

The key differences between seminars alone and long-term coaching are that coaching is a long-term effort, it involves getting in the trenches with sales professionals, and, of course, coaching leads sales professionals to do the things they don't want to do so they can earn what they want to earn.

Providing the best training for your sales professionals is good, but I don't care how much information they get. Even the most powerful lessons do no good if they are not applied. You can book the best, most-inspiring speaker, but if your sales professionals don't know what to do (or don't believe they are capable), once they're back in their respective fields, they won't retain that knowledge. At best, one-day training events will produce a shot-in-the-arm effect with a short-term boost in sales numbers.

Sales Executive Council research shows that performance increases 22% with education alone. Without continued coaching and on-the-job reinforcement, sales professionals lose 87% of the training after just one month. With long-term coaching, performance can increase by up to 88% because sales professionals retain the lessons from the seminar/educational sessions and discover how to implement them successfully and consistently. That means that the information is worth 22% alone, but your reinforcement is worth 66%.

Putting lessons into practice is easy...but it's easier not to. Just ask the former Biggest Loser contestants who have gained all their weight back. Those who succeed typically have a support system to keep them on track, motivated, and inspired. And that's where you, the sales coach, come in. Be the 66%.

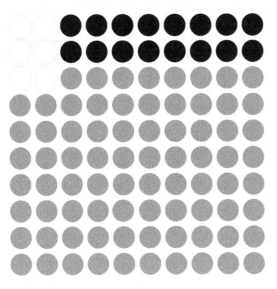

22%

Percent retention after one-day training alone

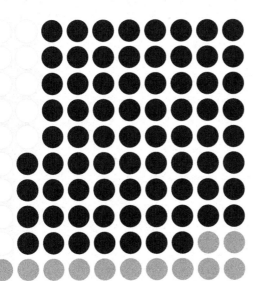

88%

Percent retention after one-day training in combination with long-term coaching

Live by the Formula for Success

Managers *focus on changing circumstances.*

Coaches *focus on increasing conversion rates.*

I don't believe in sales whisperers (sales professionals who can just sense whether a prospect is a buyer or not) or sales gods who either bless you with the numbers or don't. I believe in creating a strategy for success. To know where you're going, you've got to know where you are.

So let's do some math. You've got a goal (it goes on the left) and the factors that contribute to that are the price, monthly prospects, and conversion rates (they go on the right).

Sales Goal = Average Price x Monthly Prospect Numbers x Conversion Rate

To understand how these factors affect your success, you need to remember two things. First, as with any equation, all factors are dependent upon the other factors. For example, if you lower your price, you must increase your traffic or your conversion rate to reach your revenue goal. Second, the value on the left side must equal the value on the right side. Otherwise, the equation is not true.

Now let's plug in some real-life numbers to see it in action. If your monthly revenue goal is $1.2 million and the average unit price is $300,000, you have to sell four units to reach your goal.

But you only sell one so you check your records and see that you had 80 prospects. You sold one unit, so your conversion rate for the month was one out of 80 (1/80).

$$\$1.2 \text{ million} = \$300,000 \times 80 \times 1/80$$

Multiply all three factors on the right side (300,000 times 80 times 1/80)

$$\$1.2 \text{ million} \neq \$300,000$$

You didn't reach your goal.

To figure out why you're falling short, you've got to balance the equation. You could lower your goal to $300,000, but that would harm your company's bottom line. So let's scratch that idea.

You could lower your price to $200,000, but then you'll have to sell even more units to reach your goal of $1.2 million. **Not a good idea.**

You could try increasing your number of potential prospects. But, if it takes 80 units to make one sale, and you need four sales in a month, you're going to have to **find a way to get an additional 320 prospects.**

Okay, so quadrupling prospects and maintaining that pace every month is a ridiculous idea, no matter what kind of market you're in. So you need to turn to your last variable: your conversion rate.

Your conversion rate is 1/80, so right there you've found the reason you're falling short of your goal. **Here's the good news—your conversion rate is a factor that your team members have the power to control. But it requires you to make a choice.**

To reach your monthly sales goal, you can choose to have your sales pros:

1. Increase their traffic from 80 to 320 every month

Or...

2. Increase their conversion rate by convincing *three of the other 79 prospects to choose them.*

The key to increasing the conversion rate is creating emotional urgency in customers. And that's where you, as a coach, come in, leading sales pros to see and tap into the power of two truths:

1. That people's desire to improve their lives has more influence over their buying decision than any other factor.

2. That a sales professional has the ability to influence that desire.

When customers fall in love with a product, they will choose it over the competition, despite market circumstances. Sale pros make the difference—not price, not traffic numbers, but sales pros.

Sales teams achieve success by choosing to convert more sales from the existing prospects by building up customers' emotional urgency.

Increasing conversion rate by creating emotional urgency provides success even in tough markets. There is never a better time for prospects to improve their lives than at this moment.

Avoid the Experience Trap

Managers look for the right experience.

Coaches look for the right people.

Steve Ballmer, Microsoft's CEO, said the iPad would fail. With billions of sales and counting, it's clear that Ballmer was suffering from paradigm paralysis(*2*), or "the inability or refusal to see beyond the current models of thinking." We often do the same with resumes, saying experience is one of the most important aspects of a candidate. And then we eliminate resumes that don't have the words we're looking for, often eliminating the very people we need on our team.

This is especially dangerous when we have screeners who may be eliminating people based on their own biases. Perhaps you have a highly reluctant HR person who doesn't like aggressive salespeople and therefore ditches resumes with that word or feel.

Gallup research shows that within seven days, employers know if new hires are going to make it in their role. And yet it takes seven years to get them out of the industry. Experience can hold too much weight in our process. People may have a lot of experience and find out somewhere along the way that the career they've invested a decade in is just not for them.

I'm not against hiring experienced sales professionals, but I am certainly against having experience at the top of the qualities you're looking for. It can cause you to hire people who are not meant to be in your industry or role—people who would be happier in a different role/industry altogether.

To avoid the experience trap, consider all factors. And remember, it's easier to teach skills than beliefs. Hold yourself accountable to improving your team rather than just filling empty spots.

Reflection

1. Have you ever hired for experience only to be disappointed by the sales professional's performance?

2. If the answer is yes, then why do you keep hiring based on experience?

3. Have you eliminated people based on their resume?

Additional Reading

Psychology of Sales Call Reluctance, by George W. Dudley

2 - *mnsu.edu/comdis/kuster/infostuttering/paradigmparalysis*

"Think winter when it's summer."
—Jim Rohn

Prepare for the What Ifs

Managers prepare for the best.

Coaches prepare for the worst and hope for the best.

There is a natural ebb and flow to the market, and there are some seasons and circumstances where it's easier than others to be successful. One of the core aspects of what Jim Collins calls a "10X Leader" in the book *Great By Choice* is Productive Paranoia. This is where leaders are always thinking and preparing for the circumstances that might affect their success in the future. Having a well thought-out plan before the circumstances get tougher is key to your success as a sales leader.

If you know there is going to be a blizzard, do you bring a jacket? Yes. Just the same, if you know that some bad circumstance is inevitable, why not be prepared for it?

Creating a plan before something happens gives you an edge. It allows you to think logically rather than emotionally. When you are in the middle of tough circumstances (such as a down economy, lower prospect numbers, etc.), you will be under stress and have a higher probability of doing something irrational and/or outside of your strategy. When you're in the middle of it, it's easy to operate out of fear. On the flip side, if you know what you are going to do when the weather turns foul, then you can just execute the plan. When you prepare for any situation, you are ready for any situation.

Time is of the essence in bad circumstances. By the time you have realized that sales are down, you are already losing time coming up with a new plan. By the time you have started executing the plan, you could be several weeks behind.

Planning ahead ensures that you will keep your cool as the sales leader. Since you are the primary source of confidence in the sales team's mental attitude, you need to show your cool under pressure. If sales professionals see you sweat because you are getting worried, they will panic too.

Planning will keep you ahead of the competition so you can steal market share from them. Remember: when the market gets worse, it doesn't mean that people stop buying. It just means that there are not as many people buying.

"It is a conceptual blueprint for action: that is a perception of what should be done, where it should be done, and why it should be done. Your philosophy is the single most important navigational point on your leadership compass."
—Bill Walsh, *The Score Takes Care of Itself*

Have & Sustain Standards of Performance

Managers use the job description as their standard.

Coaches constantly lay out and maintain standards of performance.

Bill Walsh had "Standards of Performance" that outlined the specific behaviors, beliefs, attitudes, and philosophies necessary to achieve his overall goal. This single document became the compass that led him and his team to three Super Bowl wins.

The "Standards of Performance" for your team must be specific, measurable, and realistic. They must include your non-negotiables and your expectations for what excellence looks like (both for your team members and for yourself) that reflect your philosophy on success.

Benefits of Establishing your Standards of Performance:

- Takes the emotion out of decision-making during stressful and or uncertain times.
- Gives you and your team "laser focus" around these standards that, when executed, will allow the "score [to take] care of itself."

Once you present standards to your team, you must uphold them in order to maintain authority. After you've established your standards, sell those standards to your boss, your team, and your peers. Transfer your hot beliefs on the importance of the standards.

What not to do:

1. Disrespect your team members' knowledge and past experience.

2. Delay setting expectations, thinking, "I'm just going to get to know them first." Big mistake. Huge. Don't do it.

3. Ease in.

What to do:

Set expectations early and often:

Setting expectations removes ambiguity and increases accountability. To set clear expectations:

1. Stand up and set (or reset) expectations: "Here's the kind of coach that I'm going to be for you and here's what I expect from you." Whether it's your first day on the job or your thousandth, do this ASAP.

2. Every day, remind your team of one of your expected behaviors and why it is important.

3. Institute quick accountability. When expectations have been broken (on either side), there needs to be quick accountability to get the relationship back on track. If you wait too long, you risk losing engagement, credibility, and trust. You risk a perceived lowering of your standards.

4. Follow through, follow through, follow through. Once you've set up the initial expectations, make sure to follow through. It's like car

maintenance. A car will fail if you drive it without taking it in for oil changes, new tires, etc. One day, it's going to blow up on the side of the road. A car on fire is no use to anyone, but it shouldn't come as a surprise when you're 40,000 miles overdue for an oil change.

5. When patterns emerge and the adjustments and recommitments don't work, then you're gonna have to terminate some people. But setting expectations and following through will lower the need. Hint—If a person is surprised by a firing, it's your fault. It means you didn't do your part by constantly maintaining or making adjustments and recommitments.

At the Ritz Carlton, employees are required to carry the "Gold Standards" card, which states the hotel's "values and [the] philosophy by which we operate." Everybody knows what's expected of them. Bottom performers hate it because it makes it clear when they're not doing their job. But top sales professionals love it because they know what's expected of them and have a goal to reach for.

"Iceberg, dead ahead!"
—Titanic watchman

Earn Respect

__Managers__ want faux friendships.

__Coaches__ want to earn respect.

Your goal should not be to build your Facebook friend list or gain a faux friendship with your team members. You may want them to like you, but you need them to respect you. Earn respect by:

Teaching them Something New:
If sales professionals don't feel like they're learning anything from you, it will seem like a waste of their time. If you are able to pass new knowledge and information along, you will earn respect.

Solving Hidden and Admitted Problems:
Icebergs only show 10% of their Titanic-sinking potential above water. It's like that with your sales professionals, too. When they share their struggles with you, they only talk about 10% (the admitted problem). The other 90% (the hidden problem) is underneath the surface—and ready to do damage. Own the process by getting down to that other 90% and influencing the conversation rather than just participating in it. It goes like this:

So Heather, a sales professional, says she needs a Customer Relationship Management (CRM) system to keep track of her leads and make more money. That's the admitted problem. While the company may eventually provide a CRM, the hidden problem is that Heather needs to take personal accountability for her success.

So doing a little submarine dive and showing Heather the ice underneath the surface allows you to coach her in a different way. Get her to do the math and determine whether it's something that would be worth investing in herself.

If a CRM would save Heather an hour a week, is that enough time to make 100 extra calls a month? And if so, how many sales (and how much money) would that translate into? Okay, well there are CRMs for individuals that cost $5 a month. Is it worth the investment? If yes, then she can decide whether she wants to make that investment in her career or keep waiting around for the company.

It boils down to not letting Heather stop at her gut reaction of "The company needs to give me a CRM!" It's about leading her to see that she is responsible for her own success.

Or maybe Heather thinks her issue is that prospects aren't responding to her emails. You can either spin your wheels helping her write more engaging subject lines, or you can get back in that submarine and address the real issue—Heather's tele-phobia. You'll talk to her and find out she's emailing because it's more comfortable than calling. She doesn't want to call people at home because she feels like she's intruding on family. She doesn't want to call people at work because she feels like she's intruding on work. So then she just never calls.

As a coach, solve the deeper problem by leading Heather to see that she's doing her customer a favor by calling...and a disservice by not. If she doesn't call, prospects don't get a chance to ask the questions they've thought of since leaving.

Go deeper for the real issues. Address those, not what they're saying is wrong. Solve the admitted and the hidden problems.

Owning the Process:

Make it easy for the sales professional to achieve and develop. Respect their time. Know where you're trying to go. Don't just be there for the sake of being there. Go with a purpose and see how you can lead the person toward personal growth.

Be purposeful in moving them forward, getting them one step outside their comfort zone. Tell them where you're going and be respectful of their time. Top sales professionals are self-sufficient and if you're just there without an agenda, they resent you and spend the time checking the clock.

Holding them Accountable to the Solution:

You own your purpose/relationship, but they still need accountability to do what they need to do. Follow through and follow up. When you have certain expectations and commitments that you've mutually agreed upon, then there needs to be accountability if they don't do it—something in place to remind them of why they're doing it in the first place. It always needs to tie back to their goal of improving their life/achievements.

Just as they close their customers on the options they believe are best for them, you must close your sales professionals on the solutions you provide. Help them make a decision that includes the when, where, why, and leaves them saying, "Yes, I'm going to do this." If they don't follow through, remind them of their commitment and how they've broken that.

Here's the deal: If you're doing what you're supposed to do, the best sales professionals will love you (in addition to respecting you) and the worst may not like you, but they'll still respect you. You've gotta have the respect part. You can friend them on Facebook later.

"Without struggle, there is no progress."
—Frederick Douglass

Have No Fear of Conflict

__Managers__ are afraid of conflict.

__Coaches__ know that without conflict, there is no change.

T raining that doesn't change behavior is nothing more than information. Coaching takes training to the next level—providing changed results and equipping sales professionals to become the best version of themselves. It's a challenge to get your people to exceed their own expectations, but one of the most important qualities you can have to make it happen is not fearing conflict. Conflict allows you to grow your people and to build trust.

Without conflict, there is no change. I'm not talking about "make my day" kind of conflict; I'm talking about holding sales professionals accountable to doing what they're uncomfortable doing, which leads them to become the best version of themselves. As a leader, you're not doing your people any favors by enabling them to stay in their comfort zone. Conflict allows you to push sales professionals.

One of the greatest benefits of embracing conflict is that it allows you to set expectations and hold people accountable to those expectations. As counterintuitive as it may seem, this also builds trust. Take Liesel (senior vice president at a top homebuilder) for example. She knows who she is and everyone around her knows exactly what to expect from her. She has no problem with conflict—up, down, or sideways. And her assertiveness builds trust with her team and allows her to lead effectively.

There's a dangerously prominent idea that conflict equals death. We may not say it, but any time we delay a tough conversation or sweep our observations under a rug, we're denying its power. While conflict can cause our hearts to pound and sweat to gather on our foreheads, a lack of conflict cheats us out of progress and growth, leading to mediocrity and dullness (i.e., death). The coursing veins and adrenaline rush of a fierce conversation are even physical indicators of health and vitality. The contrast is to just exist. Who wants that?

Liesel clearly states her intentions and by following through daily, she builds trust with her people. People respect and appreciate that more than they do someone who uses passive aggressive communication that leaves them guessing. Or someone who sweeps issues under the table, talks behind people's backs, or doesn't address things as they come up. Liesel doesn't do that. She strikes while the iron is hot. If a behavior is not in line with the expectations, Liesel communicates about it immediately. No surprises. From the employee's perspective, it's healthy because they don't feel like they're walking on eggshells.

It's true that the criticism may be tough to swallow, but the alternative (living in fear) is way worse! If a team member is surprised when they get written up or fired, chances are, there's a lack of good, healthy conflict.

Balance is important here too—embracing conflict doesn't mean you can't give a little sugar with the medicine. As Liesel says, "Punch 'em in the face: kiss 'em on the way out."

Liesel is great about following the "expectations, accountability, and praise" method. She sets expectations, holds people accountable to those expectations, and then praises when their behaviors line up.

If it's going to benefit the people in their career, Liesel will say it. And such forthrightness is a great way to build trust.

If I had to choose an environment with too little conflict or one with too much, I'd choose the one with too much. Why? Because without it, you can't accomplish your purpose as a sales coach—to lead sales professionals to do the things they don't want to do so they can earn what they want to earn.

PART THREE

Coach the People Side

Intro to the Six Levels of Coaching

Managers focus on the circumstances.

Coaches focus on the people.

Unless you're building an iPhone, or an iAuto, your product is unlikely to distinguish you enough to bring you the profit you're looking for. So you better focus on the things that can really set you apart.

Coaches who focus on the sales process, people, and presentation are most effective at building a solid, results-oriented team. However, those who stay in the first three levels of coaching (the most common and least effective), end up falling behind the pack. Below are six levels of sales training/coaching and the characteristics of each.

Levels one and two (the shallowest) cover circumstances and results. Level three, activity-based coaching, focuses on behaviors. Focusing on behaviors is a bit more effective than the first two because it considers the activities and behaviors that contribute to success. But levels four, five, and six are where the magic happens.

Level four, process-based coaching, involves analyzing where in the process the sale got stopped and how to start it again. The sales coach may ask which product prospects are considering and what is hindering them.

Level five, presentation-based coaching, really gets down to what motivates buyers. Questions may include, "What was your selling message with the prospects?" or "Why do they need our product to improve their lives?"

As we've discussed, people-based coaching is the deepest and most effective level of sales coaching. It gets to the crux of the sales professionals' goals and the motivations that drive them to perfect their sales presentation, move prospects forward in the process, and earn what they're worth. Level six questions include: Why do you need to reach your sales goals this month?

If you were your own coach, how would you advise yourself to improve your last customer presentation? What do you hope to accomplish in your career? What part of the sales process makes you the most uncomfortable?

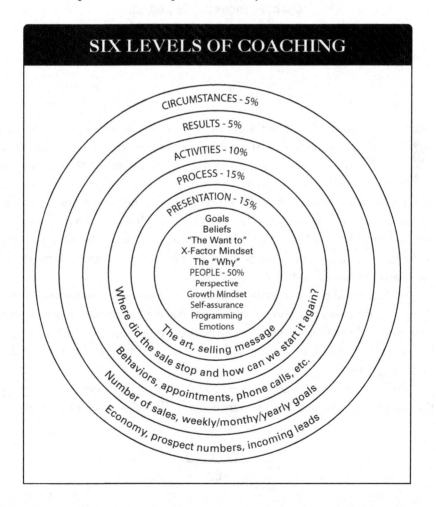

Get Permission

Managers lead by command and control.

Coaches get permission to lead.

 ou'll have more success if you gain a relationship with your sales professionals where they want your input, and a key to that is getting permission. Below are some ways you can gain permission from your people.

The Talk

The goal of the initial talk is to lay out what sales pros can expect from you and for you to gain permission to be their coach. When team members embrace your role as a coach, they will allow you to challenge them, knowing that your coaching benefits them and leads them to meet their goals. Athletes and students look back fondly on the coaches and teachers in their lives who didn't allow them to settle for less than their very best. You can be this kind of coach in your people's lives.

The script below provides a guideline, but it can be amended to fit your needs or to suit the current status of the relationship. First, establish yourself as a partner in your sales professional's success:

"I'd like to talk through the best way for me to provide coaching support for you and find out what you most need from me. I want to provide so much more than administrative support for you and I sincerely want to contribute to your success. I want us to be able to support each other doing the best job we can. So let's talk through this and commit so we can both be as successful as possible."

Let them talk first. As with selling to customers (and remember—the sales professional is your customer), you must understand the customers' needs and expectations before you present your case, and you must use the information they provide as a springboard. However, as with any customer, if they want you to talk first, then you should be prepared to do that.

This will likely be an unfamiliar exercise and they may have difficulty identifying their needs. You may need to dig a little further:

"I'd like to know which issues you feel most threaten your conversion rate and what you think can be done to overcome those issues. Talk to me about it from a face-to-face selling standpoint, and then, if necessary, from a strategic standpoint. This will allow us to put our heads together, pool our resources, and see what we can come up with."

Here are some possible questions to facilitate the discussion:

1. What do you feel you do really well in the selling process?

2. What type of customer do you relate to well?
   Note—the above two questions start with their perception of strength and affirm their bucket of knowledge.

3. What are the most difficult customers for you to deal with?

4. What objections do customers raise that make the greatest difference in your conversion rate?

5. What are the most difficult kinds of customers for you to deal with?

6. What do you need in order to reach your sales goals this month?

7. How would you describe yourself as a sales professional today and how would you ultimately like to be able to describe yourself?

8. How do you think you are perceived by most of your customers/the rest of the sales team/company management? How does that compare to how you want to be perceived?

9. What are the three things about your sales approach or your career that you would most like to improve?

10. What is your favorite part of selling and your least favorite part?

11. What is your favorite part of your job and your least favorite part?

12. Is there anything bothering you or keeping you up at night?

As the discussion progresses, be prepared to discuss your own perceptions candidly but respectfully. This can be a very important part of the sales professionals' perception of their identity. It can also be an extremely valuable conversation for them, especially when centered on ways they can improve. Hint—It's just as important for them to see your desire to improve as it is for you to see theirs, so be open to discussing the things you would like to improve if they ask, or if you feel it would add credibility or move the conversation forward.

In the first session, just listen. Take note of your sales professionals' goals or record the session so that you can be fully engaged in the moment. Conclude the conversation on a positive note:

"Thank you for sharing so openly with me. I'm committed to working with you and pooling our resources to figure out how to get you from where you are now to where you want to be as quickly as possible. If there's anything you want me to be thinking about for our next meeting, let me know. I value your time and want to keep our meetings fairly short. To make every minute count, I want us

both to be prepared. In the next session, I'd like to [pick one]:
- *Review the most recent topics from the training and how to apply them.*
- *Brainstorm on all of your prospects.*
- *Talk about one piece of your sales approach.* (See Principle 48, *Inch Wide, Mile Deep,* for more).

Some of the topics above can make fruitful group discussions as well as give a variety of people a chance to express their own experiences. You don't have to have all the answers if you have colleagues who have greater experience with a particular challenge or question.

While you are asking your team what kind of sales professionals they want to be and how they want to be perceived, consider the same questions for yourself. You are continuing to grow, just as they are.

Understand Why Your People Are Who They Are and Do What They Do

Managers think results come from the right abilities.

Coaches believe successful results come from the right beliefs.

Your people are who they are and do what they do because of their beliefs. And they have the beliefs they have because of their programming. Beliefs drive emotions, emotions drive behaviors, and behaviors drive results. I've always maintained that beliefs have more to do with success than our abilities and that the coaching along the way makes all the difference.

So getting down to a sales professional's beliefs will allow you to tap into everything else. It's a powerful thing. It's at the core of this whole book and my whole training program.

Have you ever wondered why some of your people engage and some react? It's because of what they believe. Or why some sales pros dwell on circumstances and others believe that whether they succeed or fail, it's all on them?

It's because of how they've been programmed. It's beliefs and programming that separate the top earners from the average earners.

But here's the good news: You can influence both. And that's what we've been talking about—what you'll continue to learn in the coming principles.

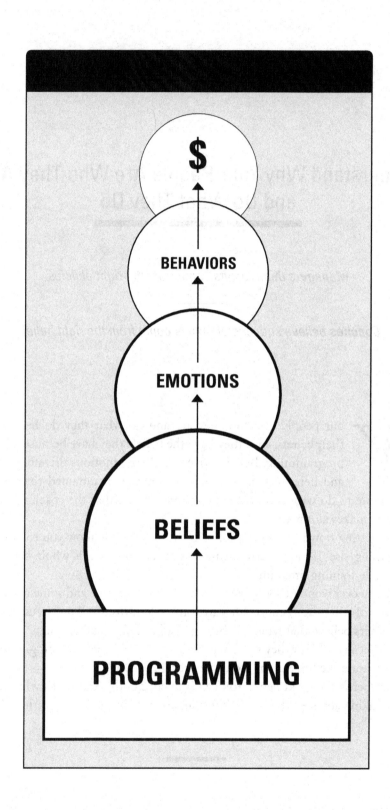

Encourage a Growth Mindset

Managers allow their people to fall victim to the lottery mindset.

Coaches teach and model a growth mindset.

H ave you seen people who put all of their paycheck on lottery tickets? They do that because they believe that they have no control of their destiny—that their life is in the hand's of karma or the sales gods. The average earner's beliefs are that they're only as good as the product, or price, or location, or market. This is a fixed mindset, lottery mentality.

On the other hand, top earners know that's nonsense and would rather invest in themselves and their beliefs and training because they believe their life is in their own hands. Top sales professionals and coaches operate with this kind of growth mindset. A growth mindset says, "What I am currently doing equals what I am currently getting. If I improve what I am currently doing, then I will improve what I am getting." What we say to ourselves and our teams can have a direct effect on creating a growth mindset or fixed mindset.

We're not born with our beliefs. We form them throughout our life and experiences. You're using your knowledge within the comfort zone of your beliefs. Without moving outside the "area of possibility," we can't grow. The coaching along the way makes all the difference in encouraging a growth mindset.

Encouraging a Growth Mindset:

Celebrate the process, even if it hasn't yet resulted in a sale. Ask sales pros to share war stories on how they've moved sales forward in the process.

If a sales pro brings in an offer, use it as an opportunity to understand what they accomplished with the buyer. Ask them questions to find out what decisions they've accomplished. If they haven't accomplished several of the decisions, talk them through it. Lead them to realize that not knowing enough about the buyer puts us in a position of weakness in the negotiation.

Example: "Thank you for focusing on the customer's buying process. You put forth a great effort and I can tell that it paid off with your new sale."

Examples of Fixed Mindset Feedback:

- *"Great job on making the sale."* (This feedback doesn't make a connection to the behaviors the sales pro has done to achieve the sale.)
- "Just write up any offer. We need sales!" (This mindset encourages sales pros to get off the process and focus solely on price. It might get you immediate results, but it confuses your team.)

It will also cost you sales in the future because you will only be able to get sales when you buy them.

You'll inadvertently cripple your sales pros if you tell a struggling sales pro to "hang in there," and that a sale "will eventually happen." This promotes the belief that it's a numbers game and has nothing to do with their efforts.

You can encourage a growth mindset in a struggling sales pro by saying:
- *"Keep putting forth the effort towards the sales process and the sale will happen."*
- *"Let's focus on what you did accomplish with the buyer so that we can celebrate those victories."*
- *"Let's focus on your last five prospects—the decisions you accomplished with them and where the sale stopped. Together, we will come up with a strategy to advance the sale."*

"If I said to most of the people who auditioned, 'Good job, awesome, well done,' it would have made me actually look and feel ridiculous. It's quite obvious most of the people who turned up for this audition were hopeless."
—Simon Cowell

Strike a Balance

Managers fall heavily on one side of the spectrum—either grit or grace.

Coaches strike a balance.

I've observed thousands of coaches and they all have a tendency to fall into one of two coaching styles—all grit (aggressively aggressive) or all grace (lacking specific, constructive feedback). You probably know right away where you fall on the scale. If you don't know, get an anonymous poll from your team and find out which direction they think you tend towards.

If you tend toward grace, you probably also tend toward generic praise like Paula Abdul on American Idol (e.g., "All you can do is the best you can do"). But it won't make anybody better.

If you tend toward grit, people may know they're going to get the honest truth and specific advice to lead them to improve. Your straight-shooting advice carries the most weight, but you also might come across as harsh and unlikable. Think Simon Cowell, whose stinging, sometimes-degrading comments drive contestants to tears.

You want to lead people to achieve their goals in life, and the only way to do that is to give them advice on how to become better. But if you're all grit, your style may be too harsh. And if you're all grace, you may be ineffective.

Effective coaching provides specific praise and advice on how to improve, but without belittling. It means providing honest, useful criticism without tearing someone down.

This sort of assertiveness is the healthy way to motivate someone and to build a productive, effective coaching relationship based upon mutual respect.

To coach effectively, you must achieve a balance between grit and grace. All grit may work with some sales professionals, but it doesn't lay the foundation for a healthy long-term relationship with your team. On the flip side, all grace may make you some friends, but it won't challenge your people or create consistent results.

Successful coaches find that balance while increasing the probability that their sales professionals:

- Will respect them.
- Will want to listen to them.
- Will have the desire to follow their advice and improve.

You need temperance either way.

STRIKE A BALANCE

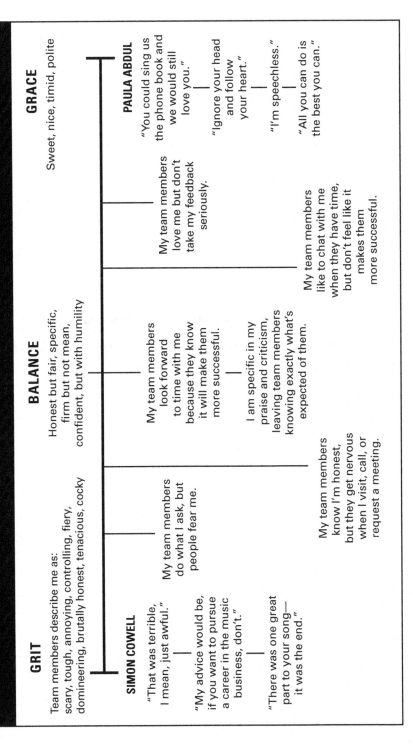

GRIT

Team members describe me as: scary, tough, annoying, controlling, fiery, domineering, brutally honest, tenacious, cocky

SIMON COWELL

"That was terrible, I mean, just awful."

"My advice would be, if you want to pursue a career in the music business, don't."

"There was one great part to your song— it was the end."

My team members do what I ask, but people fear me.

My team members know I'm honest, but they get nervous when I visit, call, or request a meeting.

BALANCE

Honest but fair, specific, firm but not mean, confident, but with humility

My team members look forward to time with me because they know it will make them more successful.

I am specific in my praise and criticism, leaving team members knowing exactly what's expected of them.

GRACE

Sweet, nice, timid, polite

PAULA ABDUL

"You could sing us the phone book and we would still love you."

"Ignore your head and follow your heart."

"I'm speechless."

"All you can do is the best you can."

My team members love me but don't take my feedback seriously.

My team members like to chat with me when they have time, but don't feel like it makes them more successful.

———————

"A man who works with his hands is a laborer; a man who works with his hands and his brain is a craftsman; but a man who works with his hands and his brain and his heart is an artist."
—Louis Mizer

Revere Sales

Managers like getting sales.

Coaches revere the science and the art of selling.

B ecause of his love and respect for the game of football, NFL Coach Bill Walsh celebrated the science and the art of a well-executed play, whether or not the play was successful. Success to him was when his people did what they were trained to do with precision. On the other hand, a play which resulted in the desired outcome, but was executed sloppily, earned his correction.

A world-class coach like Bill Walsh reveres disciplined football. Reverence is a special word, conveying an intangible but intense passion and respect for something or someone. Do you revere the science and the art of a well-executed sales process?

We could add something to Louis Mizer's quote about an artist. The best sales professionals engage at every level. Beyond the hands, brain, and heart required for artistry, selling requires being present on every level—even the soul. So a man who works with his hands, his brain, his heart, and his soul is a true sales professional. Being a good sales professional is harder than being a laborer, a craftsman, and even an artist. That's who you are leading. Do you come across to your sales professionals as someone who truly understands that? Or do you come across like someone who is managing just any department?

You'll be the most effective coach when you revere and respect sales. That's why I use the term sales professional instead of salesperson or sales counselor. It comes from my reverence for the profession.

If you revere the science and the art of selling, you'll still get sales, but you'll do it with integrity. Your sales pros will feel respected and valued. And that's a team they're going to want to be a part of.

"A return to first principles in a republic is sometimes caused by the simple virtues of one man. His good example has such an influence that the good men strive to imitate him, and the wicked are ashamed
—Niccolo Machiavelli

Create the X-Factor Revolution

Managers talk and listen to negative, circumstantial-based chatter.

Coaches create an environment where such chatter is socially unacceptable.

Social influence is a powerful thing—whether for good or for evil. As a big believer in positivity, I'd like to see it used for good—promoting a culture of self-improvement, positive attitudes, and accountability. A one-on-one with Robert Cialdini talks about the power of social influence regarding why teenagers choose to smoke, saying there are four main factors that lead to their decision:

- A history of delinquency—14% more likely to smoke
- A history of depression—14% more likely to smoke
- One or two parents who smoke—23% more likely to smoke
- Two or more friends who smoke—1000% more likely to smoke

Since there is a direct correlation between negative conversations and lack of success in sales teams, the first thing I do when I come on with a new organization is measure how much of the sales team's conversation revolves around blaming negative circumstances for hindering their sales success. I've found that such conversation outweighs talk of the things that can be controlled.

Here is the interesting part: not all members of the team feel that they are a victim of the market. A minority believe that it's up to them to find a way to sell more, but that it's socially unacceptable among their peers to speak up and say something positive.

You likely have at least one of those positive voices on your team and it's time to get them involved in leading a revolution. The climate of the sales organization is affecting your sales results whether you think it is or not. Make a commitment today to start the X-FACTOR revolution!

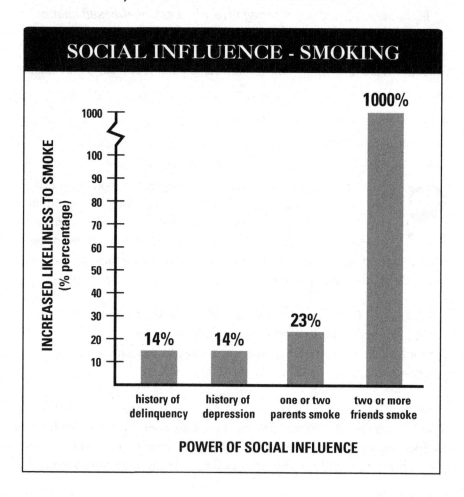

PART FOUR

Putting it All Together

"Most people don't want to be excellent at what they do. They want to be acceptable. They may say they want to be excellent, but they're not willing to do what it takes. They don't see the point."
—Rich Tiller, author of *Motivation from the Heart*

Hold Your People Accountable

Managers have to constantly prod to get people to
achieve the minimum expectations.

Coaches hold people accountable to becoming
the best version of themselves.

Accountability is about committing ourselves to stay above the circumstances in our thinking and our doing every day.

There are four steps to accountability, and they go along with gaining the "want to" relationship with your people. Because until your people see the value of you holding them accountable to being the best version of who they are, you're going to be operating in the "have to." And there's only so much you can do from there. As a coach, you play a role in teaching and coaching your sales professionals through each of the following steps:

Awareness: The first step for your sales professionals is to be aware that they are not the best version of themselves in every area. This is usually an easy part of the process. What's harder is the next step: accepting that something needs to change and having an interest in changing. And perhaps most importantly of all—that they can't do it on their own. That's what they say in Alcoholics Anonymous, isn't it? You have to admit you have a problem and that you need help. Well, that might be a little extreme for our situation, but it still applies. It's harder than just being aware that something could change. It's accepting that you need to do something about it to cause the change.

Step three is another relatively easy one: making a plan to make the sales pros the best version of who they are. This should be done together.

And finally, the hardest (and most important) step is execution—following through on the plan.

Now it's true that we can't teach what we don't know and we can't hold people accountable to a standard we're not familiar with, but don't get caught up in that. While it doesn't mean you have to be better at executing those behaviors, it absolutely means you must master the playbook and know the expected behaviors better than anybody else. That way you can easily see the difference between the actual behavior and the playbook behavior.

If you don't want to hold people accountable in the way described above, then you're gonna have to lower your standards. Take a minute to digest that thought. Ambitious leaders often start off with high expectations they believe they are capable of; they write them down, give them a fancy name, proclaim them to their team...and never talk about them again. And then they get frustrated when people don't live up to them.

I will never recommend you lower your standards. There's always another way.

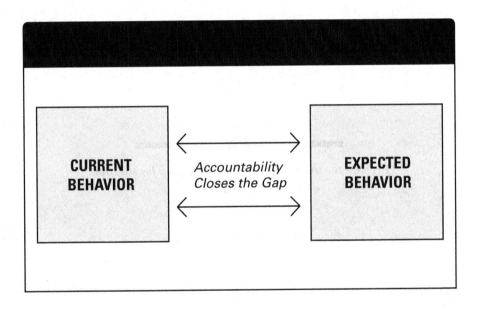

CURRENT BEHAVIOR ← Accountability Closes the Gap → EXPECTED BEHAVIOR

"Prepare the child for the path, not the path for the child."
—Unknown

Give Roots and Wings

Managers overregulate.

Coaches instill accountability by giving team members wings.

C ongrats, you've made it. When you got your title, chances are you didn't know how to coach. It's not that you couldn't, you just didn't have the tools yet. Well now you do. You have the title along with the know-how.

So give yourself a pat on the back and think about all you've learned. You have the special gift and responsibility to really affect people's lives.

Remember—our beliefs have more to do with our success than our abilities, and the coaching along the way makes all the difference. You are that coach. You are that leader who has the ability AND the responsibility to see more in people than they see in themselves. Take this power with reverence and respect because with great power takes great responsibility.

It's time to lead. It's time to grow your people. It's time to do more than just teach your sales pros what to do in each situation. It's time to give them roots and wings.

Denis Waitley describes it in the poem, "Roots and Wings:"

If I had two wishes, I know what they would be

JASON FORREST

I'd wish for Roots to cling to, and Wings to set me free;
Roots of inner values, like rings within a tree,
and Wings of independence to seek my destiny.
Roots to hold forever to keep me safe and strong,
To let me know you love me when I've done something wrong;
To show me by example, and help me learn to choose,
To take those actions every day to win instead of lose.
Just be there when I need you, to tell me it's all right,
To face my fear of falling when I test my wings in flight;
Don't make my life too easy, it's better if I try,
And fail and get back up myself, so I can learn to fly.
If I had two wishes, and two were all I had,
And they could just be granted, by my mom and dad;
I wouldn't ask for money or any store-bought things.
The greatest gifts I'd ask for are simply Roots and Wings."

Teach the science and coach the art so that sales pros can make the process their own. Is it hard to provide a balance between self-assurance and regulation? Sure. But it's possible.

You must set expectations, but also let your people surprise and delight you. It's a worthwhile journey. And if you do this, you will be able to look back on your life and be able to say, "I made a difference in people's lives." People will tell your kids how you mattered to them—how you believed in them enough to coach and invest, how you improved their lives.

Your sales coach,
Jason

ONE FINAL NOTE

Thanks for sharing some of your valuable time with me. If you believe that the philosophies presented here will increase your probability of reaching your goals, give us a call so we can talk about your next steps.

CONTACT US AT:
Info@ForrestPG.com
www.ForrestPG.com
1-888-391-4326